$\mathcal{B}$EAUTY $\mathcal{L}$AB

by Mildred Leinweber Dawson

HOW SCIENCE IS CHANGING
THE WAY WE LOOK

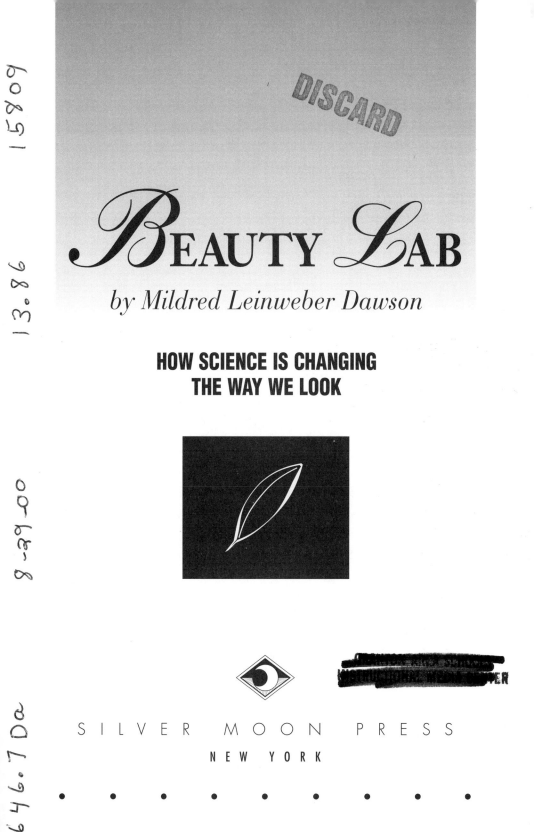

SILVER MOON PRESS

NEW YORK

First Silver Moon Press edition 1996

Copyright © 1996 by Mildred Leinweber Dawson

For information write:

Silver Moon Press
160 Fifth Avenue
Suite 622
New York, NY 10010
(800) 874-3320

Design and cover photograph by Geoffrey Notkin
Edited by Sarah V. Frampton
Photographs on pages 3 and 17 courtesy of Neutrogena
Photograph on page 45 by Matthew Jordan Smith
Photographs on pages 4 and 33 courtesy of Index Stock Photography
Photographs on pages 10, 24, 60, and 69 by M. Bryan Ginsberg
Photographs on pages 38, 52, and 57 by Clifford Keeney
Medical illustrations on pages 28 and 41 courtesy of Parlay International

Library of Congress Cataloging-in-Publication Data

Dawson, Mildred Leinweber
Beauty Lab/by Mildred Leinweber Dawson.
p.   cm. — (Science Lab series)
Summary:Provides information about skin, eyes, hair, teeth, and fitness
to enable the reader to make the most of his or her appearance.
ISBN 1-881889-84-X : $13.95
1. Beauty, Personal–Juvenile literature. 2. Health–Juvenile literature.
[1. Beauty, Personal. 2. Health.]
I.Title II. Series: Science Lab
RA777.D38   1996
646.7'2—dc20
96-314
CIP
AC

10 9 8 7 6 5 4 3 2 1

Printed in the USA

TABLE OF CONTENTS

Special Thanks to:

Dr. Addie Ganik, Jazzercise, Dr. Robert K. Maloney,
Dr. Vincent P. McMahon, Dr. Ronald H. Ruffle,
Salon de Sabina, Dr. Avery M. Scheiner,
Dr. Tara Sexton, and Nancy Varise

for their help in preparing this book.

For my parents and brother, my husband and children,
and for Gareth.

—M.L.D.

INTRODUCTION

Health and Beauty, Hand in Hand

"Jessica? Are you up here? It's almost time for dinner."

Jessica held her breath until she heard her mother's footsteps walking back down the stairs. Then she exhaled a stream of smoke out the bathroom window, threw her cigarette stub in the toilet, and sprayed the room with air freshener.

She brushed her teeth, put on some perfume, and unlocked the door. On her way out Jessica glanced in the mirror. She admired the new sweater she had bought at the mall that afternoon.

She was so busy covering her tracks and admiring her new clothes that she missed a few things. Things like lines under her eyes from too little sleep, yellowing teeth from too much coffee and too many cigarettes, and dry skin from last season's trips to the tanning salon.

All in all, not quite the sophisticated look this sixteen-year-old was hoping for.

Throughout this book, you will encounter many people—kids like Jessica who make choices that affect their appearance and even their health. You'll discover that if you treat your body well, it will return the favor.

You will also meet researchers who have discovered some of the ways certain systems in our bodies work and what steps we can take to look and feel good.

Thanks to the efforts of medical and cosmetic scientists, we now have many new choices in beauty treatments. Research in such areas as skin, hair, teeth, and eyes have led to many valuable new products, drugs, and medical techniques that can help us look our best. These products and techniques often let us preserve the original beauty of our bodies—and sometimes improve on nature. To appreciate the natural beauty of our bodies, just think of babies: the glow of their complexions, the brightness of their eyes, and the soft shininess of their hair.

Many new cosmetic treatments perform with extraordinary effectiveness. Unlike earlier generations, we now have drugs that can minimize, and sometimes cure, acne, and others that can grow hair on bald heads. And, if our eyesight declines, we can choose extremely comfortable contacts and eyeglasses.

It is important to remember that cosmetic choices are often medical choices and may have serious effects on our bodies. To evaluate and choose beauty treatments wisely, we need to understand how the body's systems work.

This book will help you to gain that knowledge.

In addition, this book will give you insights that will help you be a smarter consumer of cosmetic products. You will learn how to look at beauty advertisements and identify honest claims from overblown or even false ones. This knowledge will help you save time, effort, and, best of all, money.

Anthropologists tell us that the pursuit of beauty and the desire for decoration are found in nearly all societies. They believe the desire to beautify the body is a human need as basic as our needs for love and security. Makeup actually dates back to the time of cave-dwelling Cro-Magnons, who lived about 25,000 years ago. (At that time, facial paint was worn mostly by men as a way to scare off evil spirits and human enemies.) Despite local laws against "excessive adornment," even the Puritan women of colonial Massachusetts wore makeup and dyed their hair.

The quest for beauty may have occurred in all places and ages, but we now face issues unknown to past generations. One new challenge is the continuous attempt to stay physically attractive as our lives extend far longer than they ever have before. This lengthening of our life expectancies is an important cosmetic issue. Think of the wrinkles we may have to deal with if we really do start living to age 130, as some scientists believe we may.

In the late 1700s, the average American could expect to live between thirty-five and forty years. By 1900, average life expectancy increased to forty-seven years. In this century, life spans have stretched even further, and by 1992, the average life expectancy had reached seventy-two for men and seventy-nine for women! Previous generations died before their teeth fell out and their skin turned leathery, but we will live to see these changes, so we have to take conscious care of our bodies. If we preserve our complexions and smiles now, we can avoid many years of wrinkles and dentures.

However, another beauty challenge for us today is to stay sensible about our body care. In America, beauty is a megabusiness, worth many billions of dollars. Cosmetic companies sell romance and dreams along with lipstick and creams.

It's great to be able to take responsible pride in your appearance, but obsessing over your body is a mental drain and can even become dangerous. You perform best when you feel happiest with yourself. Yet many people unfairly compare themselves to models who devote their whole lives to dieting (often unhealthily), exercising, and creating faces that look flawless in photos.

The truth is, our faces and figures will undergo many changes as we pass through the different stages of our lives, even though we will probably try to minimize or delay certain changes. Nearly every teen gets pimples, just as most middle-aged people have some wrinkles. However, no one should endure serious acne without medical relief. And many wrinkles, we now know, can be prevented by avoiding the sun. Likewise, teenagers often go through awkward stages while their bodies are shifting from childhood to adulthood, and few forty-year-olds have the bodies they had in their twenties. But with enough exercise to build strength and grace, we can all look better. No one's body can be flawless, but science is continually making it easier for us to look attractive and feel good about ourselves.

However, it is important to be realistic when setting beauty goals. If we have a physical problem or feature that truly distresses us, then we may want to address it. We might tweeze out bushy eyebrows or have a beauty mark removed surgically. Of course, the only person who should decide to fix a physical characteristic is you. There is no set of rules for determining what is beautiful—after all, actress Brooke Shields was proud of her heavy eyebrows, and model Cindy Crawford made a beauty mark (a mole) her trademark. We brighten our own lives, and others' lives, when we feel we look our best. But always remember, our character is far more important than our appearance. As the actress Claudette Colbert said, "It matters more what is in a woman's face than what is on it." ◆

CHAPTER 1

Your Skin, the Sun, and Oil

Jason, age fifteen, tossed and turned miserably in bed, unable to sleep. He had spent most of the day baking on a chaise lounge in his backyard. His acne had been bothering him and his friend Ben had said that the sun dried up pimples. It had not worked, though. His blemishes were as bad as ever, and now he had a vicious sunburn, too. Jason shifted about uncomfortably, wishing he had never listened to Ben.

As our largest organ, the skin deserves our understanding and respectful care. Laid out flat, the skin of a 150-pound person covers twenty square feet and weighs nine pounds! Yet many people don't realize that their skin is such a vital organ, as important as their brain or their ears. Here are just a few of the things your skin does:

- It acts as a barrier to keep toxins (poisons) out of your body.

- It is a vitamin D factory. Vitamin D helps your body absorb calcium, which you need for healthy bones and a strong heart.

- As your largest organ of sensation, it acts as a warning system. If you get a splinter, the pain tells you to remove it before the area becomes infected.

- It surrounds and protects your delicate inner organs, like a peel protects a banana.

The look and feel of your skin often mirrors your internal state—to have a healthy complexion you must be in good physical and emotional health. Maintaining your complexion requires basic skin sense, especially about the sun. Extreme weather conditions and rough handling can injure skin, but nothing does as much damage as sunlight.

Skin sense starts with understanding the composition of your skin's three layers: the epidermis, the dermis, and subcutaneous layer.

The layer you see is the epidermis. In most places, it's about as thick as one page of this book. The very top of the epidermis consists of flat, dead, and dying cells called keratinocytes. They're named for the keratin in them, which makes the skin tough and waterproof, and provides some protection from the sun. Keratin exists only in the epidermis, hair, and nails. We constantly shed dead epidermal cells in tiny flakes.

The basal layer of the epidermis contains pigment-bearing cells called melanocytes. Melanocytes produce tan, brown, or black pigments that help determine our skin's color. All people, no matter how fair or dark, have about sixty thousand melanocytes per square inch.

The depth of your skin color reflects the size and shape of these cells, the amount of pigment they produce, and the distribution and color of the pigment. Black people usually have evenly distributed, dark pigment. While in white people, the pigment is lighter and some of it is often clumped together in freckles.

Below your epidermis lies your dermis, the skin's middle layer. About as thick as fifteen to forty pages of this book, the dermis contains blood vessels, nerve endings, sweat glands, and oil glands. When functioning normally, the oil glands pour the right amount of oil into the deep narrow pockets, or follicles, from which hair grows. There are hairs all over your body, except on your palms, soles, nipples, and parts of your genitals. Most are soft, downy hairs called vellus hairs. The darker, coarser hairs on your head, underarms, and pubic areas (if you've undergone puberty) are called terminal hairs. Oil called sebum travels up the hair and out onto the surrounding skin. The sebum lubricates the hair and spreads, forming a film to keep your skin soft by preventing the evaporation of water.

The dermis also contains collagen and elastin, two kinds of protein fibers that are arranged in regular patterns. Collagen and elastin give your skin its strength, spring, and adaptability.

The innermost layer of your skin is its subcutaneous layer. Made up of mostly connective tissue, blood vessels, and fat cells, this layer protects the body from injury and helps it retain heat.

What makes skin beautiful? Well, people have always wanted smooth, clean complexions, but tastes among some people have changed over the years. From ancient Rome all the way up to the early 1900s, fair-skinned women desired the palest complexions possible. During these centuries, some women went so far as to paint their faces with a dead-white, lead-based makeup called ceruse. Even after science revealed how potentially deadly this beauty regimen was, women continued to use it.

In the 1920s, tan skin became the rage for some Caucasians, and by the 1950s, many people aimed for the deepest tans possible. The Little Miss Coppertone ads were first presented in Miami in 1953. "Don't be a pale-face!" she urged, and Americans listened. Unfortunately, some people still bake in the sun today despite scientists' warnings that 90 percent of skin cancers result from too much sun.

Cancer experts also say that 80 percent of the sun's damage happens before the age of twenty. Melanoma, the deadliest skin cancer, will probably strike more than 34,000 Americans in 1997, and it will kill more than 7,000.

The sun poses the greatest threat to fair-skinned people with light eyes who almost always burn and rarely tan at all. People with skin in the middle ranges are less susceptible but still need to take precautions by always wearing sunscreens. In fact, even deep brown skin can burn and develop cancer and should be protected by sunblock during periods of long, intense exposure.

How does the sun do such severe damage? And how can you protect yourself?

The sun's energy comes to us in various forms, like heat and visible light. The sun also emits three types of invisible ultraviolet (UV) rays. These are called UVA, UVB, and UVC rays.

UVA rays greatly outnumber UVB rays and reach us on Earth at constant levels, no matter what the season or time of day. UVA rays deeply penetrate the skin, affecting the dermis. Scientists have recently found that UVA rays, along with UVB rays, can greatly harm the skin and promote skin cancer. Within the past ten years, researchers have discovered that UVA rays act as an accomplice, helping UVB rays to do their damage. UVA rays also damage your eyes, leading to blinding cataracts, and change your immune system's ability to fight disease. Therefore, it is very important to wear UV protective sunglasses when you're in the sun.

Scientists best understand UVB rays, which cause the most sunburns. They are strongest during the summer months, and between the midday hours of 10:00 A.M. and 2:00 P.M. These rays penetrate the epidermis and damage it, causing premature aging in the form of wrinkles, leathery skin, and dark spots.

UVB rays also scramble the DNA in your epidermal cells. DNA passes hereditary information from one generation of cells to the next and controls the cells' production of protein. The UVB rays confuse the cells, mixing up the instructions that tell them how to behave in a healthy way.

Scientists believe that DNA scrambling is one way that UVB rays contribute to skin cancers and to beauty problems often wrongly attributed to aging, such as spots and wrinkles. In fact, an incredible 80 percent of the visible changes the skin undergoes are due to the sun's impact.

Currently, UVC rays do not reach us on Earth. Instead, they are blocked by an atmospheric layer consisting of ozone gas. This ozone layer, though, has been dwindling due to the effects of several types of pollution. Various laws have been passed to try to reverse ozone depletion, but if more is not done to save the ozone layer, greater amounts of UVA and UVB rays will reach us, increasing the cases of skin cancer. Without an adequate ozone layer, UVC rays may soon reach us as well.

Fortunately, we have lotions and oils called sunscreens, or sunblocks, to protect ourselves. There are two types of sunscreens. Some are physical blocks to keep out the sun's rays, like zinc oxide, the white cream you sometimes see on a lifeguard's nose. These simply reflect and scatter the sunlight. Most sunscreens, however, work through chemical means. They contain special ingredients that absorb UV rays before they can harm your skin.

Sunscreens are rated with SPF numbers (for Sun Protection Factor). The SPF number tells you how long you may stay in the sun before you will begin to burn. This rating system is not perfect, though, and the actual amount of protection depends on how much lotion you apply, how hot or windy it is, and how much you sweat. Always choose a product with an SPF of at least 15, but don't pay a lot more for one rated 30 or 45 as scientists have determined that the additional benefit is minimal.

Many of today's sunscreens contain ingredients that block only UVB rays. However, sunscreens that protect the skin from both UVB and UVA are available. These are the ones you should choose and use every time you go out in the sun. According to the Food and Drug Administration, a branch of the federal government, "regular and liberal" use of sunscreens is very important. The damage done by the sun accumulates bit by bit throughout your lifetime. Most of it occurs when you least expect it--while walking to school, riding your bike, or just hanging around outside. Your lips are especially sensitive, so remember to apply a lip balm that contains a sunscreen.

Sometimes people want a tan look without the risk of photo-aging (sun damage). Science has made this possible

Remember that the sun can burn you whether you're sitting on the beach or playing outside. So, be certain to apply plenty of sunscreen whenever participating in your favorite outdoor activity.

with self-tanning creams. These cosmetics, which temporarily dye the skin, first came onto the market about twenty years ago. QT (for quick tan) was one of the first, but it turned people orange. Self-tanning creams that have been available for the last seven years are much more refined and natural looking. Remember, though, even if you use these creams you still need a sunblock when you go outside. Self-tanning creams will darken your skin, but they won't protect it from the sun.

If you're still going to tan, despite all the damage it could do to both your appearance and your health, at least take these precautions, which will help, but will not eliminate the risk:

• Tan gradually

• Apply sunscreen

• Never frequent tanning salons. Exposure to UV light is never safe.

Now that you know how to protect your skin from an external threat, the sun, let's talk about a problem that starts from within, acne. What causes acne and how can you best handle it?

Excess oil is the major culprit. When it's functioning the way it should be, the skin is literally a well-oiled machine. Oil glands in the dermis, also called sebaceous glands, make oil, or sebum, which they pour into the deep narrow pockets (or follicles) in which hairs grow. Every follicle is lined with cells, and when the skin's condition is normal, these cells die and fall off into the follicle gradually. Oil and dead cells flow up and out of the follicle through an opening called a pore on the skin's surface. Once there, the oil mixes with sweat and spreads out thinly and evenly to keep the skin moist.

However, oil doesn't moisturize directly. Instead, since it prevents evaporation, it acts as a barrier to trap water within the skin. That's why the best way to put on moisturizer, which usually contains oil, is to wash your skin, leave it damp, and then apply the lotion or cream.

When you're a child, your sebaceous glands produce just the right amount of oil, and your skin is moist and generally blemish-free. Then at puberty, your body starts producing greater amounts of hormones called androgens. These reach the skin through blood vessels in the dermis. In boys, the testes generate these hormones. In girls, the ovaries and adrenal glands (which sit on top of the kidneys) do so.

Oil glands can be very sensitive to androgens and often respond to them by making excess oil. This excess oil can become trapped within hair follicles if it's blocked by plugs of sticky cells. The sticky cells accumulate when the follicle grows and sheds its lining cells too quickly. Bacteria that are always present in the skin then breed among the entrapped oil and dead cells. The bacteria become more numerous than normal, and blackheads and whiteheads form. Pimples and cysts may soon follow, often on the face, chest, and back.

Pimples arise when the hair follicle starts to leak, having been weakened by its excess burden of oil, dead cells, and bacteria. This leakage can irritate the dermis, which often leads to redness and swelling.

The depth at which a follicle leaks into the dermis determines the amount of pain and the potential for scarring that may come with the pimple. A follicle that leaks deeply within the dermis and sheds a lot of oil can cause a cyst, the worst kind of acne. A cyst occurs when a wall forms around the leaked fluid, causing a painful, hard lump. Many cysts require medical treatment because they can often leave scars.

Few people enjoy a blemish-free adolescence; 80 percent of teens have acne to some degree. Your gender and ethnicity help determine your tendency toward acne. Usually boys have acne more often and more severely than girls do. Teens of European descent are more acne-prone than those with African or Asian roots.

Family history comes into play too. While acne itself is not inherited, members of your family may have oil glands that are more sensitive to hormones than the members of your friend's family. What this means is that the same amount of hormone may provoke a bad outbreak in the Green sisters but cause no problem for the Fisher brothers. There are no certainties. Don't assume that just because your mom had bad acne, you will too.

At the same time, it's not a bad idea to find out about your family history. If your case is mild and not likely to get worse, you will probably be fine with over-the-counter remedies. If you think mild acne is likely to get worse, though, you should see a dermatologist (skin doctor). The doctor can be of most help when your acne is in its early stages and still highly responsive to treatment. If you postpone treatment you may increase the chance of permanent scarring.

How can a dermatologist help? And how has acne treatment changed and improved since your parents were teenagers?

Doctors have recognized for a long time that the key aspects of acne treatment may include: (1) controlling the overactive oil glands, (2) destroying the bacteria that cause infections and inflammation, (3) reducing the hormonal contribution to the problem through hormone treatments, and (4) reducing the plugging of the follicles that traps oil and harmful bacteria. The ways in which dermatologists do this have changed significantly since your parents' adolescence.

Years ago, doctors used to advise people with acne to avoid chocolate, French fries, and other greasy foods. Today, doctors don't believe that diet makes much difference when it comes to pimples. Although that stuff does negatively affect your health! Also in the past, acne treatments used harsh drying techniques; strong soaps, lotions, and alcohol toners. These sometimes helped mild acne, but they did little to improve more serious cases. Strong drying agents could also leave the skin red, rough, and chapped.

Other treatments doctors used included X rays to slow the activity of the oil glands and UV rays to cause peeling. Today, these methods are considered much too dangerous — they can lead to skin cancers.

Today, if your acne is mild to moderate, the doctor will often suggest gentle cleansers and mild antibacterial lotions. These often contain benzoyl peroxide. This drug, which has been in use for over twenty-five years, kills bacteria within the follicles. It also causes slight peeling, which helps the pores to open and empty themselves. Sometimes, doctors also prescribe oral (taken by mouth) antibiotics, to help control the bacterial aspect of the problem.

For severe acne that does not respond to these methods, doctors now have a drug called Accutane, which is often highly effective. Accutane, also taken orally, belongs to a group of drugs called retinoids. Retinoids reduce the tendency of the follicles to shed their lining cells too quickly. This helps to reduce the formation of plugs in the pores.

When Accutane entered the pharmaceutical (medicinal drug) market in 1982, it was viewed as the first major breakthrough in dermatology in more than twenty years. Accutane can often clear up severe acne completely in a sixteen-to-twenty week course of treatment. If a patient doesn't respond to the drug the first time it is used, the doctor may prescribe a second course of treatment, which often works.

Doctors and patients must use Accutane cautiously. It can have serious side effects, including headaches, mood changes, and severe stomach pains. Most importantly, anyone taking it should not become pregnant because it is teratogenic; it can badly damage a fetus. Any woman taking Accutane must abstain from intercourse or use contraceptives. The drug can also dangerously affect the fat content of blood and the workings of the liver, so a patient's blood and liver functions must be checked carefully while he or she is taking it.

Another dramatically effective way dermatologists can help acne patients is with cortisone, which is injected directly into very obstinate pimples. This treatment can clear up or drastically reduce a bad blemish overnight.

Dermatologists offer a few points of advice if you have acne. First, don't wash too much. Teenagers often wrongly equate having acne with being dirty and wash their faces constantly. This is irritating to the skin and can actually worsen the problem. Also, don't pop them! Squeezing pimples just spreads and multiplies the infections in your skin.

No matter what, take hope: When you're in your twenties and thirties, after the peak acne years, your skin will again produce the right amount of oil. Eventually, your oil glands will grow tired and produce less oil. This can lead to the dry skin and fine lines that people begin to see in their forties, so believe it or not, one day you'll be using moisturizer every night instead of pimple medicine!

When Jason told his parents why he'd let himself get so sunburned, they decided it was time to consult a dermatologist about his acne. The doctor prescribed a mild cleanser and an antibacterial lotion and explained to Jason the importance of protecting his skin from the sun.

Jason's skin improved noticeably with the new regimen, although his acne didn't go away completely until he reached his twenties. Jason is pale, but handsome, and he understands proper skin care.

His sun-worshipping friend, Ben, never learned those lessons—and had to have a skin cancer removed during his freshman year in college.   ◆

CHAPTER 2

Chapter Two: Eyes–Looking Out, Looking In

Keisha, her friends agreed, was a horse fanatic. She loved riding them, grooming them, and even talking to them. But when she was fifteen her doctor prescribed glasses for her for the first time. She tried to ignore how uncomfortable they were when she was riding, but they were a big distraction. They slid off her nose when she got sweaty and bounced around when the horse cantered. Most of her friends wore contacts, but they didn't seem to work for Keisha. She couldn't see clearly enough with soft lenses, and hard ones would never work. A trotting horse would kick up dust that could get trapped beneath them.

So Keisha was intrigued when she read about surgery

that could permanently correct nearsightedness. She and her parents decided to investigate.

If you agree with most Americans, you value your vision above all your other senses. Our eyes are our most important organ for finding out about the world. We use them constantly. Think about what they do for us:

- Each eyeball is only one inch in diameter, yet its flexibility is enormous. It lets you see the period at the end of this sentence and a huge star trillions of miles away.

- When people say, "I can't hear as well without my glasses," they're right. Our eyes give all kinds of visual clues that enhance our understanding of what we hear.

- Just as each of us is left- or right-handed, so too are we left- or right-eyed. Most people constantly favor one eye when they aim a camera.

Your eyes might be large and round or small and almond-shaped. They may be the palest blue or the darkest brown. Their color depends on how much of the pigment melanin they contain and how deeply it's embedded. Dark eyes have lots of melanin close to the surface; pale ones have little melanin, deeply embedded. Perhaps your eyes are framed with nearly invisible lashes, or with a jet-black fringe. No matter what they look like, they are an animated, vital feature of your face and a particularly important source of information. The sixteenth-century French poet Seigneur Du Bartas called the eyes "the windows of the soul," and many poets since have expressed similar thoughts.

Even if you see perfectly today, at some point you'll probably have a vision problem that you will want to correct. If you have less than perfect vision right now, your choices are glasses, contact lenses, or surgery. More than half of the U.S. population wears either glasses or contacts (141 million out of a total population of 245 million). The choice you make will affect both how well you see and how you look. Choosing wisely requires a basic understanding of how your eyes function and how they can malfunction. It also requires familiarity with the different options available.

Our eyes don't actually let us see objects. They let us see the light reflected by objects. Each eyeball sits in a protective cone-shaped cavity in our skulls. The fat-padded cavity is called an orbit or a socket.

The outer layer of the eyeball is covered by two kinds of tough living tissues. One tissue is the sclera, the white part surrounding five-sixths of the eyeball. The other tissue is the cornea, the clear part that covers one-sixth of the eyeball, the part we see and the part beneath our lids. Like all living tissues, the cornea needs oxygen. However, it lacks the blood vessels necessary to bring it oxygen dissolved in blood. So instead, the cornea takes oxygen directly from the air, from the tears that bathe it, or from the blood vessels that surround it.

The cornea covers the colored part of the eye (the iris) like a watch crystal. It lets light enter through the black hole known as the pupil, in the middle of the iris. The cornea also starts the process of bending (or refracting) light rays that enter the eye, a job that is finished by the lens. Controlled by muscles, the pupil constantly changes size to regulate the amount of light entering the eye.

You can observe this yourself. Take a mirror and sit by a lamp, preferably one with a dimmer. Turn the light on and off, or gradually change its brightness, and watch your pupils enlarge and shrink in response.

Behind the iris lies the lens. The "lens" got its name from its resemblance to a round lentil. Clear and about the size

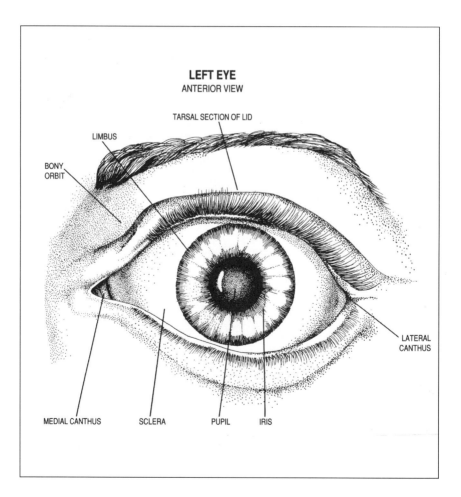

LEFT EYE
ANTERIOR VIEW

TARSAL SECTION OF LID

LIMBUS

BONY
ORBIT

LATERAL
CANTHUS

MEDIAL CANTHUS   SCLERA   PUPIL   IRIS

of an aspirin, the clear lens focuses light toward the back of the eye, where the retina is. The retina is the innermost layer of your eyeball and is as delicate as a piece of wet tissue paper. It contains light-sensitive cells called rods and cones (because of their shapes). These cells absorb the light rays that pass through the lens and convert them into electrical signals. The electrical signals, in turn, travel along the optic nerve to your brain.

For vision to be sharp, light rays entering the eye from an object must meet precisely at a single point on the retina. If the rays don't meet precisely, vision is hazy. Problems in the eye's ability to focus light rays on the retina are called refractive errors. These cause blurred vision and are among the most common of all physical ailments. They afflict more than one hundred million people in the United States. The following are the three refractive errors that occur:

- If you are nearsighted, your eyeballs are elongated from front to back, or your cornea is too steeply curved. As a result, light rays passing through your pupil converge (come together) before they reach the retina. You can see things that are close but you can't see things in the distance very well. The medical term for nearsightedness is myopia.

- If you are farsighted, your eyeballs are compressed from front to back, or your cornea is too flat. As a result, light rays entering your eye through the pupil pass through the retina without having converged on it. You see distant objects clearly but can't see nearby objects well. Doctors call farsightedness hyperopia.

- If you have an astigmatism, your corneas are misshapen. This causes the light rays from an object to focus in more than one spot. Your vision is blurry. People who have an astigmatism often have other visual problems as well.

Refractive errors usually start when people are still in school, but they may show up either at birth or not until adulthood. Eventually, all of us will wear eyeglasses because we will develop presbyopia, a form of farsightedness that affects almost all people by the age of fifty.

Several different kinds of specialists help people with refractive errors:

1. Opthamologists are medical doctors. They can prescribe eyeglasses or contact lenses and perform corrective surgeries. They also diagnose and treat eye diseases, but their specialty is surgery.

2. Optometrists examine your eyes to evaluate your vision, and they can prescribe glasses and contact lenses. They also diagnose and treat most eye diseases and then refer you to an opthamologist if necessary.

3. Opticians are technicians who dispense the eyeglasses and contacts lenses that are prescribed by opthamologists or optometrists.

Opticians and some optometrists work in stores where eyeglasses are sold; many opthamologists in the United States are affiliated with eyeglass stores; opthalmologists and some optometrists work in offices, clinics, or hospitals.

As mentioned earlier, there are three kinds of solutions for visual defects: eyeglasses, contact lenses, and surgery. Eyeglasses are by far the oldest. They were invented in the thirteenth century, and used in Europe and possibly in India and China. At first, eyeglass lenses were made of transparent stone or glass, and frames were made of metal, horn, or bone. Some of the first eyeglasses were an expensive status symbol, but they weren't easy to use. They didn't have long side pieces, as modern glasses do. Instead they were held in place by hand or balanced on the nose.

In the sixteenth century, inventors tested different ways to secure eyeglasses to the face. They tried leather frames and straps, cords wound around the ears, and metal spikes that attached to the wearer's hat. Finally, in 1728, a London optician invented eyeglasses with side pieces that pressed against the head. Curved pieces that fit behind the ears, like those we use today, weren't around until 1880.

Plastic was also invented in the late 1800s, but high-quality plastic lenses weren't introduced until 1948. Scratch-resistant coatings were created in the 1970s, and since then plastic lenses have gotten tougher, thinner, and lighter. The assortment of frames now available in plastic, tortoise shell, and metals is unprecedented. Today, many people think of eyeglasses as a fashion accessory. Some people buy many frames to match different outfits and moods.

Contact lenses, plastic disks worn directly on the eye, were invented about one hundred years ago. They started to become popular during the late 1950s and early 1960s. A force known as surface tension holds them in place; it's the same force that holds raindrops on a windowpane.

Contact lenses do a better job of correcting vision than eyeglasses do. Since they move with your eyes, they offer a more natural field of vision. This keeps things sharp not only when you look forward, but also to the side. Contacts may also eliminate certain distortions that can occur with eyeglasses, and they don't fog up, get wet, slide down your nose, or bounce when you exercise.

Twenty-eight million Americans wear contact lenses—two times as many as just ten years ago. In 1994, Americans spent $1.8 billion for contact lenses. Most people with visual problems can use them. Only about 10 percent of people with refractive errors have problems that contact lenses simply won't correct.

At first, the only contact lenses available were hard ones. Hard lenses are made of a rigid plastic called PPMA (polymethyl methacrylate). When they're in place, oxygen reaches the cornea through tears that are pumped beneath the lenses during blinking. It takes people days or even weeks to get used to hard lenses, and they can be painful when dust or dirt gets trapped under them. They also tend to pop out and get lost. Doctors rarely prescribe old-fashioned hard lenses today because the newer types are healthier. In fact, only 1 percent of contact lens wearers in the United States still have hard contacts.

Soft contact lenses reached the market during the 1970s. They are made from hydrophilic (water-loving) plastics, which absorb water. Oxygen can pass directly through them so the cornea can breath; this keeps the lenses comfortable. Their softness allows them to stick closely to the cornea so they don't trap dirt and rarely pop out. Most

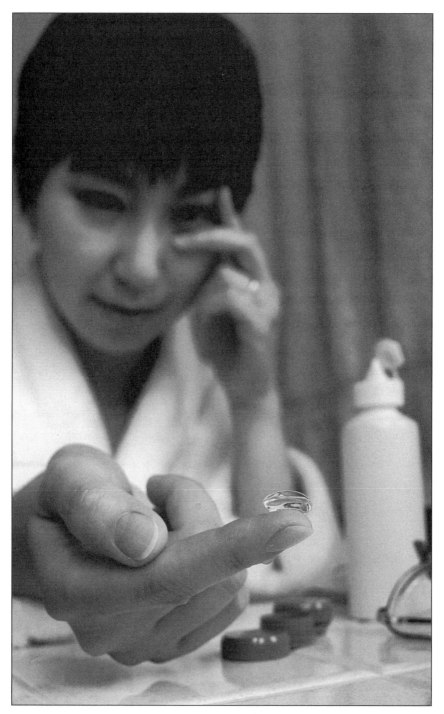

Contact lenses offer a more natural field of vision than glasses do. It is estimated that 28 million Americans wear contact lenses.

people adjust to soft lenses quickly—usually within a week or so. Although soft lenses usually correct vision sharply, they don't always do so—especially for people with an astigmatism. Eighty-four percent of contact lens wearers in the U.S. choose some form of soft contacts.

Another option for people who want both comfort and sharp vision is the use of rigid gas-permeable (RGP) lenses. These became available in 1979. Although they are hard, they allow oxygen to pass freely to the cornea. These take more time to adjust to than soft lenses—about three to four weeks—and can sometimes pop out. Fifteen percent of contact lens wearers in the United States choose RGP lenses.

Hard, soft, and RGP lenses are all designed to be worn during the day and removed at night. They all require careful daily care and cleaning. When contacts were first becoming popular, wearers had to use separate solutions to clean their lenses, disinfect them (kill germs), and remove the protein deposits that can make them cloudy. Today it's much easier to care for contacts properly with solutions that serve more than one purpose. Researchers have even developed solutions that do all three jobs, making lens care that much easier.

After a certain period of time, you must also replace your lenses in order to avoid irritating protein build-up. Proteins, which are naturally present in tears, accumulate on lenses. This can make vision cloudy and the lenses uncomfortable. Most people who wear soft or RGP lenses generally replace them after one or two years. Contact lens manufacturers have even introduced lenses that are disposable after one wearing.

In 1988, the Food and Drug Administration approved the sale of extended wear-lenses. These are marketed under the premise that they can be worn, day and night, for up to six days and then thrown away. However, recent studies have strongly suggested that wearing any lenses for extended periods of time is too risky. People who sleep in their lenses have a much greater chance of developing an inflamed cornea which can cause permanent eye damage. Corneal inflammations sometimes develop after only one night of wear, so many experts strongly discourage the practice of sleeping in contact lenses. In fact, there is an eight times greater risk of corneal inflammation associated with sleeping with lenses.

Some people with perfect eyesight wear tinted contact lenses just to change their eye color. They may collect them in different shades the way others collect lipsticks. Tinted lenses have been available since the mid-1980s and, over time, have grown more natural looking through improvements in the techniques used for their design and manufacture. Translucent tinted lenses act like colored cellophane and can change light irises with a transparent wash of color; usually blue or green. Opaque lenses act like paint and cover the natural eye color. They can tint even dark eyes from brown to green or blue.

Tinted lenses can also disguise eyes that are disfigured with scars or other blemishes. People with refractive errors may also choose to wear them for cosmetic reasons. If you wear tinted contact lenses, you should be careful because they can reduce peripheral vision (vision to the side), especially at night.

One day, researchers may develop materials that really do make contacts safe for long periods of wear. Scientists may devise materials that will allow much greater passage of oxygen to the cornea. Lenses made of these materials might be so comfortable that you wouldn't even know you were wearing them. Thus, those who wear contacts might be able to keep their lenses in for even longer periods than they do today.

Surgery to correct refractive errors is by far the newest of the solutions available today. Radial Keratotomy (RK) is the oldest surgery used. It was developed in the 1970s.

RK can correct nearsightedness or an astigmatism. During the operation the doctor cleans the eye, numbs it with an anesthetic, and then cuts slits in the cornea. The slits, resembling the spokes of a wheel, flatten and reshape the cornea. Usually, this allows the cornea to focus light precisely on the retina.

Doctors perform about 500,000 RK operations each year on patients with a moderate degree of nearsightedness or an astigmatism. Also, the patient's vision has to have stabilized (stopped changing). This usually happens between the ages of twenty and thirty.

The second most popular operation is called automated lamellar keratoplasty (ALK). ALK can treat severe cases of nearsightedness better than RK can, and it also works for moderate levels of farsightedness. In ALK, doctors use a tiny machine that sits right on the patient's eye and automatically shaves off a thin layer of the cornea. ALK is performed in the United States about 10,000 times a year.

Opthamologists can't guarantee that these surgeries will give a patient perfect vision. Sometimes an operation must be repeated in order to achieve the desired visual accuracy, and sometimes the patient still needs thin glasses to see perfectly. However, statistics show that in 95 percent of cases, RK or ALK patients are satisfied with their vision and can give up glasses or contacts for most of the day.

A recent ten-year study showed that RK is generally safe. As with any operation there is a small chance of infection. While such surgical complications are rare, there was one significant negative finding about RK: People who have had RK experience the farsightedness of aging sooner than those who stick to glasses or contacts.

Opthamologists are now experimenting with lasers to perform corrective eye surgeries. They hope that lasers will be more accurate and cause less premature farsightedness. It is predicted that laser surgery will replace radial keratotomy. Every day, advancements are being made in this area, and laser surgery may soon be antiquated by a technique called LASIK, which is more predictable and has a faster healing time.

Keisha learned more about corrective eye surgery, and she, her parents, and her doctor decided that she was an excellent candidate for the operation. She had to wait until she was twenty-three, when her vision had stabilized, and then she underwent RK. The surgery went well, and the results were excellent. It was worth the wait.

Her biggest problem after the operation? Getting used to perfect vision. ◆

CHAPTER 3

Teeth and the Science of Smiling

At thirteen, Ned mostly kept to himself. He rode his bike, read, and played computer games for hours. He never stayed after school for sports or clubs, but he got good grades in all of his classes that did not require class participation. He told his parents he hated speaking in class. In fact, he rarely spoke at all outside of his home.

His parents worried about his shyness. They couldn't understand why their bright, good-hearted son was alone so much. He was attractive too. He had inherited his dad's dark curly hair and big brown eyes.

Unfortunately, he also got his dad's crooked teeth.

"A smile is the curve that sets everything straight," says comedian Phyllis Diller. How did your smile start?

When you were a toddler you had twenty baby teeth. By the time you reach maturity, these will have been replaced with thirty-two permanent teeth. Each tooth has a crown, the visible part above the gum, and a root, which anchors the tooth in your jaw.

Enamel, the pearly white material that covers the crowns of your teeth, is the hardest matter in your body. Dentin, a solid yellow substance, fills most of the interior of each tooth (both crown and root). The dentin shows through the enamel, giving most people's teeth a slightly yellow tint. At each tooth's inner core is its pulp, containing blood vessels and nerves. The blood vessels bring in nourishment and the nerves transmit sensations of extreme temperatures and pain.

Did you know that your teeth barely meet when you chew? The nerves in the periodontal ligament around the roots of your teeth let you sense the contact of opposing teeth as they grind your food. You reflexively (without thinking) adjust the movement of your lower jaw so your teeth don't gnash together. Without this reflexive action, your teeth would be ground down to nothing by the time you were thirty.

Your teeth and gums are vulnerable to harmful bacteria, which thrive on food residues that can build in your mouth. Food particles, saliva, and bacteria combine to form plaque, a sticky film. Plaque gathers and hardens on the teeth and under the gum line. The bacteria in it digest the food, producing harmful acids and toxins that can eat away at enamel and destroy gum tissue. Erosion of enamel leads to cavities, which can eventually destroy your teeth. Gum inflammation can also lead to serious periodontal disease. This can cause tooth loss. Even healthy teeth can fall out if they're not firmly anchored in strong bone with healthy gums. Most children who lose teeth do so because of decay or injury, but in people older than thirty-five teeth usually fall out because of bone and gum disease.

Although dentistry, as we know it, is a fairly new profession, people have always sought dental treatment to

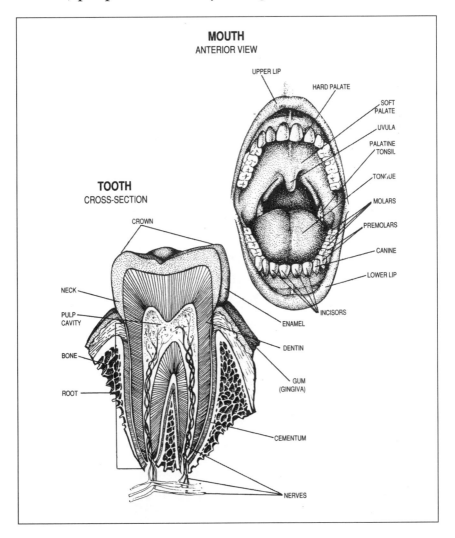

maintain oral health and to look their best. The Talmud, an ancient Jewish text, mentions tooth replacement, and archaeologists found two false molars in Egypt's Great Pyramids. Mayan people adorned their teeth by filing them into ornate shapes and applying jade inlays. Mouthwashes have also existed for thousands of years. The ancient Greeks swished away bad breath with mixtures of white wine and licorice-scented anise seeds.

If you needed dental treatment during the Middle Ages, you would have turned to a jeweler or barber. Dentistry did not become a distinct profession until the late 1700s. At that time, a major book describing dental methods and devices was published, and a man named John Greenwood invented a new drill. Run by a foot pedal, the drill reached speeds of up to 100 revolutions per minute and became an important dental tool. Today's standard drills make more than 500,000 revolutions per minute.

The invention of general anesthesia in the mid-1800s further advanced dentistry. Dentists used anesthetic drugs—such as nitrous oxide (laughing gas)—to put people into a deep sleep so that they could endure dental work that would otherwise have been unbearable.

The major problems of the first professional dentists, preventing tooth decay and loss and making patients comfortable enough for treatment, still concern dentists. Thanks to scientific advances, however, these areas are much easier to manage, so dentists can focus their attention on other areas. To the greatest extent ever, dentists can now help their patients achieve attractive smiles; teeth that not only work well, but also look great and last a lifetime.

Before we explore the new materials and methods used

in cosmetic dentistry, let's consider the progress that made anesthesia and decay easier to handle. Today, general anesthetics, which put you to sleep, are rarely used. Instead, people usually receive local anesthesia for dental work. This way, painkillers dull sensation only in the area being treated. Cocaine was the first local anesthetic used in dentistry—in 1884. In 1904, Dr. Alfred Einhorn synthesized novocaine, which was not as potent as cocaine but far less toxic. Novocaine faded from use in the 1940s, eclipsed by lidocaine, which provokes fewer allergic reactions. Today, dentists choose among several kinds of anesthetics and can control the speed with which the numbing takes effect and wears off.

Someday, you may be able to use electronic devices to control your own dental anesthesia. Researchers are experimenting with a method that involves giving the patient a small battery-powered box to hold. Wires running from the box lead to small pads placed in the mouth. The patient adjusts the current sent through the wires. The current, in turn, stimulates oral nerves and makes them unable to sense pain.

What about progress in treating and preventing decay? Throughout history, decay has been the major dental problem. During colonial days, many Americans lost at least half of their teeth to decay before age twenty. Today, there are three keys to a healthy smile. The first two are a sensible diet and a commitment to dental hygiene. As Americans have improved their diets and hygiene, their dental health has improved. But many people still suffer some degree of tooth decay and resulting tooth loss. A 1988 survey found that half our population aged sixty-five to seventy-four had lost between seven and eleven of their teeth. This is quite a lot since there are thirty-two teeth in a full set. Many adults do, though, have their wisdom teeth (the molars farthest back) extracted, leaving them with only twenty-eight.

The third key to dental health is regular visits to the dentist. Just as the toothpaste advertisements tell us, the best way to prevent tooth decay is to brush, floss, and see your dentist for cleaning and a check-up. These habits also help to keep your gums healthy, which will make your smile even nicer. Puffy, red, irritated gums make teeth look darker while bright, tight gums reflect well on teeth, making them look bright, too. At your checkup the dentist will probably ask about the fluoride in your diet and apply fluoride to your teeth.

What is fluoride? Why is it so important? Dentists have long recognized that fluoride is a major contributor to strong teeth. Current research shows that fluoride is even more important than scientists had first realized.

Fluoride, now the active ingredient in most toothpastes, was first recognized as a tooth strengthener in the 1930s. Researchers at the time noticed that people raised in areas with water containing natural fluoride had far fewer cavities than people in areas without fluoride in their water.

This observation led to widespread experiments. Communities tried adding small amounts of fluoride to their water. When tooth decay declined in those places, other cities began fluoridation programs. Today, half of all Americans drink fluoridated water.

Within the last five years, dental researchers have begun to realize that fluoride has lifelong, and daily, effects. It's not just that children who consume fluoride develop

*Good oral hygiene cannot guarantee a smile as beautiful as this girl's.
But it is an important first step in preserving the smile you have.*

strong enamel that withstands decay. Every day, a person's teeth fight the breakdown (decalcification) of enamel by bacteria in plaque. But if enough fluoride is present, it can remineralize, or rebuild, the teeth so they won't decay.

Gum chewing has gained a new respectability through recent fluoride research. Dentists now consider the chewing of sugarless gum to be a healthy practice. Chewing encourages the mouth to pour out more saliva, which is loaded with minerals, including calcium and fluoride. Minerals flow through saliva into even hard-to-reach areas of the teeth, strengthening them.

Sealants are an important new material that dentists use in their battle against decay. Dental sealants, which first came into use in 1971, are made of clear plastic. Dentists apply them in a liquid form to the chewing surfaces of the back teeth, where decay usually strikes. The sealants then harden, forming a smooth plastic barrier that keeps food and plaque out of the tiny pits and cracks common in back teeth. These openings are so tiny that not even a single toothbrush bristle can reach inside them. Sealants allow many children to grow up free of decay. In 1990, surveys showed that half of American children who visited their dentists were cavity-free. In 1980, only about a third were.

When cavities do occur today, dentists have better materials with which to fill them. In fact, dentists have better materials for nearly all the tasks they face. Once, only ugly metals and fragile porcelains were available to fill cavities, fix broken teeth, and disguise stains. Now they can work with a wide range of plastics, strong new forms of porcelain, and resins. Resins are mixtures of ceramic substances and polymers.

Some of the new materials are strong enough to withstand the rigors of chewing, so they can be used even on the grinding surfaces of molars. They can also be blended in many tones. Dentists can match the hundreds of shades of natural teeth, from pearly ivories to yellowed beiges to slightly gray tones. Improved materials and greater choices have led to a rise in cosmetic dentistry.

What are the main kinds of cosmetic problems dentists treat? And how are they treated?

Tooth fractures are a common problem for children and teens. Kids break their teeth in car accidents, through athletic injuries, falls, or sometimes even by chewing ice. Using your seat belt and wearing protective gear while participating in sports will reduce your risk. When chips to the teeth are minor, the dentists can simply file the edge smooth again. Sometimes more extensive repair is needed. Then the dentist can use bonding, laminates, or crowns.

Bonding first came into use in the 1970s. In bonding, the dentist etches the surface of the affected teeth so they will better grip a soft material that is to be applied and then hardened. The early bonding materials hardened quickly, so the dentist had to work fast. They were also likely to stain and were difficult to polish. Today's materials are better. They are highly polishable, less prone to stain, and can be kept soft and pliable for as much time as the dentist needs to create the desired look. Bonding costs about $150 to $600 per tooth.

Bonding lasts five to seven years and then must be repeated. If you have bonding done, you will also have to be careful to avoid hard foods as well as ones that promote stains. Because of the etching of your teeth during the roughening process, bonding is sometimes irreversible—it needs to be replaced but cannot be removed without showing the roughened surface.

Another new solution for fractured teeth is the application of laminates. These thin layers of porcelain or plastic have been used for about twenty years and are similar to false fingernails. Applying laminates is more expensive and complicated than bonding. However, the porcelain laminates are more lustrous, translucent, and natural looking than either bonding or plastic laminates. They cost about $350 to $1000 per tooth, last for seven to ten years, and are irreversible. Dentists also use little caps called crowns which are placed over a broken or disfigured tooth. For crowns to be fitted, much of the underlying tooth must be removed. Bonding, laminates, and crowns can also be used to correct misshapen or stained teeth.

Discoloration or staining is a very common problem. Teeth naturally darken and dull with age. They also tend to stain if people smoke or drink a lot of grape juice, red wine, coffee, tea, or cola. A new and very popular solution to staining is dentist-supervised home bleaching. For home bleaching, the dentist makes a clear, flexible plastic mold of your teeth and then gives you a special gel to place in the mold. You wear the gel-filled mold for several nights while you sleep. The improvement usually lasts two to three years before the bleaching needs to be repeated. Experts say you should not use bleaching kits that are sold without a prescription.

Bleaching is not for pre-teen children. If you are under thirteen, bleaching can be too uncomfortable because you have large pulp chambers that make your teeth more sensitive. More importantly, some experts worry about the long-term effects of bleaching. They fear that the repeated use of carbamide peroxide, the active bleaching ingredient, may temporarily damage the pulp and even heighten the risk of oral cancer. To make sure you bleach your teeth safely, proceed only under your dentist's supervision. Follow his or her instructions closely to avoid overuse of the bleach.

Another problem for many kids is crooked teeth. Doctors call this malocclusion. Malocclusion is a cosmetic problem, but also a functional one, caused by a lack of space or teeth that have rotated or shifted from their normal positions. A small jawbone may be unable to handle all the teeth growing in it. In an overly large jawbone, teeth may come in with large gaps between them.

The best and most lasting solution for malocclusion is orthodontia—the use of braces to move the teeth into better alignment. High-tech materials have improved orthodontia, just as they have improved dentistry. Old-fashioned braces that your parents might have worn consisted of metal bands circling the teeth, to which wires were attached. As the wires were gradually tightened, the teeth shifted into alignment. In the 1950s, 1960s, and early 1970s, the bands and wires were usually stainless steel. Today, braces are made of metal alloys much like those used in communications satellites launched into outer space. These alloys allow the braces to exert lighter, more even, more continuous force on the teeth, and make them much more comfortable.

Nowadays, braces are sometimes made less visible through the use of nonmetal materials, ceramics, or plastics. Orthodontists also use magnets to push teeth apart or force them together.

Computer imaging is a recent innovation that can give you an idea of how your improved mouth is likely to look. The orthodontist or dentist uses a video camera to record your present smile. He or she can tell the computer about the planned changes and about your predicted growth. Then it produces an image that predicts the improved appearance. Although this technique is growing in popularity, it is not a guarantee. Your actual post-treatment teeth may not match the image exactly.

There is one thing to remember if you are considering cosmetic dentistry. Even if there was such a thing as a "perfect mouth," you wouldn't want it because it wouldn't look natural. As with any cosmetic changes, the most important standards are your own. Your smile should make you happy.

"Was it worth it?" Dr. Perry held the mirror up to her patient's mouth.

Ned ran his tongue over his teeth, newly freed from eighteen months of braces. Nervously, he opened his mouth. Slowly, he smiled.

"Yeah." He grinned. He looked again, his smile widening. "Definitely!" ◊

CHAPTER **4**

Feeling Fit,
Looking Fine

T ara never thought about exercise. She hated the pressure of sports, with everyone waiting for you to make a basket or score a goal. She was always sure she would drop the ball or send it into the other team's net. After school, she just went home and watched TV.

She didn't think about her diet much either. She'd grab a couple of doughnuts for breakfast, and then feel so guilty she'd skip lunch. Then she'd be starving by the time she got home, so she'd finish half a bag of cookies while watching TV. Of course, by dinnertime she was stuffed.

We're all born with the urge to move, and with good natural instincts about food. But millions of Americans grow up with awful habits and don't pay enough attention to exercise and nutrition. Many recent studies have shown that Americans are sitting around more than ever. Instead of eating a variety of simple, wholesome foods, many people are getting fat by eating lots of rich, overprocessed, and packaged ones. Bad habits like these sap your energy, ruin your health, and wreck your appearance. How can you avoid them?

First, learn about fitness. Then put what you know into practice. Our fitness needs—basically an active life and a simple diet—date back four million years to the time when we evolved as a species. A species is a distinct group of animals. Anthropologists say that the first humans had to be active—finding food and shelter was serious work. The bulk of their diets consisted of plants that they gathered.

All humans are born with the urge to move. Sports, such as rowing, swimming, and running, are all fun and can lead to a long, healthy life.

Hunting brought in an occasional feast of meat, but it came from lean wild beasts, not fat farm animals.

For millions of years, people continued to be active. Until the Industrial Revolution, in the early 1800s, most people had physical jobs, and since there were no cars, most people walked or rode horses. Until recently, when TVs, computers, and video games arrived, free time was often spent outside.

As we have grown less active at work and play, our diets have moved away from simple plant foods to include far more animal foods and fat. The result has been that many people in industrial countries, including children, have less muscle and are fatter than ever.

No one should want a fat, flabby body, and most people can keep themselves in good shape by practicing a few simple fitness habits. Some of the predisposition to gaining weight is inherited and certain people have a harder time losing weight than others. But most of the time it is harder to lose weight as you get older, so it's important to get in shape when you're young.

What does it mean to be fit? There are two basic levels of fitness. The first and most important level for most of us is health-related fitness. This is the level you need to reach to look and feel well. If you stay at this level, you will greatly reduce your chances of developing certain diseases, including heart problems and diabetes. The second level of fitness is a higher one, which athletes need for peak performance.

Exercise is worth the time and effort it takes, and it takes both. Most people, adults and children, who exercise regularly report many immediate benefits. They find that it's fun to exercise, and it makes them feel more energetic and less stressed. They even sleep better. Research has found that there are lots of other good "spillover" effects from exercising. For students, better grades are one. Exercisers are also more likely than nonexercisers to practice good health habits in other areas. One survey showed that they are much more likely to quit smoking and to cut down on red meat and caffeine.

The benefits of good fitness include:

- Increased agility (the ability to bend and twist freely), which lends grace to your movements.

- Added strength, which allows you to lift things and climb stairs more easily. It also improves your posture by keeping your spine correctly aligned and your abdominal muscles tucked in (this makes you look better too).

- Increased stamina, which keeps you from feeling tired.

- Strong cardiovascular condition, which means your heart (a muscle) and lungs work better.

- Healthier body composition—less fat tissue and more muscle.

- Greater bone density, which reflects bone strength.

Heredity, or family tendencies, determines many aspects of

your physical fitness. Nearly all of those aspects, however, can be improved if you exercise enough and eat well.

What does it mean to "exercise enough" and "eat well"? These are research questions that have been hot topics for about the past thirty-five years. Many questions remain to be answered about fitness. For instance, no one can prescribe the exact amount and type of exercise you should do to live as long and as healthfully as possible. But there are certain fitness facts that have been proven again and again.

First, experts agree that you are better off doing some exercise than doing none, and the more you do (up to a certain point), the greater the benefits. They also say that lifetime patterns for physical activity are set in childhood, so if you start out as an active person, you are more likely to remain one.

Ideally, you should get twenty to thirty minutes of vigorous exercise five—or at the very least three—times each week. The exercise you choose should work your large muscles in your legs and arms. When you speed up your heart rate, you will strengthen the muscles of your heart. When you breathe faster, you improve your ability to use and transport oxygen because you are requiring more of it over an extended period of time. This kind of exercise is called aerobic exercise.

Some vigorous exercises are fast swimming, running, and bicycling. Moderate ones include dancing and brisk walking. Activities like gardening and bowling are considered gentle exercises.

If exercising almost daily sounds like a lot, it is! But you can and should work toward this level gradually. It's helpful to set short-, medium-, and long-term goals and to make them ones you can really achieve. For instance, instead of setting your long-range goal at "losing ten pounds," which may not be possible by diet alone, set it at exercising moderately four times a week. For an intermediate goal, try to exercise moderately two times a week. As a short-term goal, you might decide to cut your TV time in half and work out with a friend twice a week. Even if you never reach an "ideal" level of exercise, you'll be more active than you would have been if you'd never started an exercise program.

Whatever level you choose, keep it fun. Pick a couple of sports you like and alternate them. And, as with anything else, don't go overboard. Pick at least one day to rest. Too much of anything can be unhealthy.

What about "eating well"? Nutritionists tell us that this means eating a wide variety of fresh, simple foods. In 1992, the U.S. Department of Agriculture issued its newest food pyramid, which you can often find on the back of cereal and pasta boxes. The pyramid is a simple guide to good eating habits. It shows that you need lots of certain foods and very little of others.

Complex carbohydrates like cereals, pasta, rice, and breads provide easy-to-burn energy, vitamins, and minerals. These form the pyramid's base, which means you need the largest number of servings of these foods—six to eleven a day. That sounds like a lot, but keep in mind that the recommended servings are usually very small so it is easy to meet the requirements in a couple of meals. Keep in mind that those made from whole grains are best.

Fruits and vegetables, also complex carbohydrates, form

the pyramid's next layer. Most Americans don't eat enough of these. Aim for five or more servings a day. Many studies have shown that the people who eat the most fruits and vegetables are the least likely to develop heart disease or certain cancers.

Protein sources come next. These include dairy products like milk and yogurt, along with meats, nuts, and tofu. Your body needs proteins to build and repair structures, like muscles and bones, and to make substances like hormones. Your growth also depends on enough dietary protein. However, most Americans eat twice as much protein as they need. Every day you should have two or three servings of dairy foods and two or three of

These children are enjoying hiking. In addition to exercise, a diet which includes complex carbohydrates, proteins, and a very small amount of fats and sweets is necessary for good health.

the other proteins. Low-fat sources such as skim milk and lean poultry are healthiest.

Fats and oils, at the top of the pyramid, are important nutrients. They carry certain vitamins into the blood for shipment to their final destinations. Unfortunately, most Americans eat far too many fats. You get fat in many foods—even in breads and produce—so nutritionists suggest you use "obvious" fats like butter or oil as little as possible. Avoid animal and other fats that are solid at room temperature, like lard.

Sweets are simple carbohydrates and are also at the peak of the pyramid. Cookies and candy have no nutritional value, so limit them to an occasional splurge. Although studies show that the vast majority of American children eat sugar products daily, try cutting down as much as you can. Once or twice a week would be best.

Now you know the basic "DOs" of exercising and eating for fitness. If you do all of the above, you're likely to have strong muscles, good posture, and the kind of confidence that comes only to people who take care of themselves.

There are also some "DON'Ts" to observe. Decades of research have identified smoking as a key cause of cancer and heart disease. Many people don't realize that smoking is also harmful to your looks. Cigarettes stain your teeth and make your breath, hair, and clothing smell foul. Smoking, along with sun exposure, also leads to premature wrinkling of your skin. Excessive drinking of alcohol also destroys both fitness and beauty.

And remember, exercise and diet are only healthy when done responsibly. Everybody needs some fat on their body.

Becoming compulsive about diet and exercise is not only very unhealthy—it can kill you.

Tara's mom became concerned when Tara was panting after climbing one flight of stairs. She took Tara to the doctor, who declared there was nothing wrong that some exercise and a good diet couldn't fix. He also decided that Tara's mom could lose some weight, and guessed correctly that the whole family was out of shape.

That night, Tara's mom threw out all the junk food in the house, to the dismay of Tara's little brother. The whole family took a mile walk before dinner, and after a month they were up to four miles, three times a week.

Six months later, Tara had lost eight pounds. She still had a slice of pizza every now and then, but she knew that was okay. She was still exercising and generally eating sensibly. She had never felt better. ◆

CHAPTER 5

Hair . . . How You Want It, Where You Want It

For Carmen, age sixteen, life was one bad hair day after the next. She had inherited her mother's thick, dark, curly locks, but she longed for straight, blond hair like her friend Carol's. Carmen grew her hair long and then both straightened and bleached it, resulting in stiff, unnatural, brittle hair. At her mother's suggestion, Carmen turned to a good hairdresser, who recommended that she change not only the way she handled her hair but also the way she thought and felt about it.

You can alter your hair more easily than you can alter any other physical feature of your body, and a new hairstyle can make a great difference in your appearance. It can accent your best facial features and downplay or hide others.

People have been braiding, cutting, dying, and otherwise changing their hair since prehistoric times. Archaeologists have found hairpins and ornaments for the hair dating back to the New Stone Age, which began around 8000 B.C. The Angles and Saxons, early Germanic peoples who invaded Britain in the fifth and sixth centuries A.D., dyed their hair green, blue, and orange. The Gauls, in the fourth century B.C., who lived in the region that later became France, preferred bright red.

In the late nineteenth and early twentieth centuries, several important new processes for styling hair were introduced. In the 1870s, a Frenchman, Marcel Grateau, invented the marcel wave–deep waves set with hot tongs. German-born Charles L. Nessler invented the first permanent wave around 1905. His method took twelve hours and cost hundreds of dollars. In 1930, the cold wave, an easy, inexpensive method for perming hair without heat, was invented.

Today, consumers have a greater choice of products to dye, curl, straighten, color, condition, and otherwise change their hair than they have ever had before. In deciding which ones to use and what styles to wear, it's helpful to understand your hair. Everyone's hair varies in size, color, texture, and density. Hair is amazing!

The hair growing on us and all other mammals sets us apart from other creatures. By helping mammals maintain steady body temperatures, hair has allowed us to occupy more different kinds of environments than any other animal group. Like shade, hair provides coolness; like a blanket, it provides warmth. Temperature regulation is no longer an important job for hair, but we still have hair all over our bodies, except on the soles, palms, nipples, and parts of the genitals.

Hair can have a vast psychological impact. In many cultures, how you wear your hair speaks volumes about you. It can reveal your age (little girls may wear pigtails and elderly women, buns) or your marital status. Many cultures require married women to cover their heads; in China women used to have their hairlines plucked and heightened when they wed. Your hair may show your religious and even your political beliefs. For instance, Jamaican Rastafarians wear dreadlocks to show their respect for God, and hippies of the 1960s wore long hair as a form of rebellion.

How does our hair grow? And what accounts for all the splendid variations in the color and texture of the hair that crowns our heads? Each threadlike hair grows from within a narrow baglike structure, the follicle, which extends deep into the skin's dermis. At the bottom of the follicle, the root of the hair is nourished by blood vessels, which provide raw materials for growth. Hair growth takes place in a part of the root called the bulb.

Cells in the bulb divide quickly. New cells from deep down push out older cells. As these older cells move up, cells called melanocytes transfer pigment to them, providing color. The hundreds of shades of hair we see result from the mixing of only two pigments. People usually have some of each. Eumelanin is brown-black, and phaeomelanin is yellow-red. Subtle variations and highlights in hair color result from both the amount of each pigment within, and the thickness of, the individual hairs.

As the older cells move up, they begin to harden in a process called keratinization. Through this process, ten different kinds of special proteins, called keratins, are linked together to produce the tough, elastic strand we know as hair. Hair is tough and stretchy—a single strand can support a weight of two and a half pounds, and can stretch one-third of its length without snapping. All the hair above the region of keratinization is called the shaft.

The nature of the links between the keratin proteins decides whether the hair will be curly, wavy, or straight. In straight hair, the bonds linking the proteins run straight across. In curly hair, the bonds zigzag. If you cut straight and curly hairs crosswise and study them under a microscope, they look different. A cross section of a straight hair is round; one of a curly hair is flat.

At any particular time, 90 percent of the hairs on your head are growing. The other 10 percent are either "resting" before they continue to grow, or have died and are about to be shed. Hairs that do fall out are then replaced with new ones.

Each hair shaft consists of three layers of cells. The central core is called the medulla. Around it lies the cortex, where the pigment that decides the hair color resides. The outer layer, or cuticle, consists of flat scales layered like the shingles on a roof. The condition of these scales greatly affects how your hair looks and behaves.

Philip Kingsley, a world-renowned hair expert, explains that the cuticle cells must be clean and lie flat in order to reflect the most light, and it is their ability to reflect light well that makes hair look shiny and beautiful. When the cuticle cells are dirty and damaged, they lift up and separate, scattering light instead of reflecting it clearly. Then hair looks dull and lifeless.

The way you treat your hair when you comb and brush it affects the cuticle. Hair is very delicate and more easily broken when it is wet. Experts warn that rough treatment and overbrushing can snag the hair, causing breakage and split ends. Split ends can also come from using a blow dryer, curling iron or another form of heat on your hair. Brush your hair gently, and only enough to style it—then stop. It's better to use an inexpensive plastic brush than a highpriced one with natural bristles. The latter has too many bristles packed too closely together, which can actually break your hair.

Shampooing your hair properly and with the correct shampoo is the first step in maintaining a healthy cuticle that will shine. How often you wash your hair is a personal preference. Each of your hair follicles contains an oil gland, and the oil produced to coat each hair shaft keeps the hair soft. During puberty these glands, like those in your skin, may be overactive, causing your hair to feel too oily. If this is the case, a daily shampoo may help.

With the huge variety of shampoos available, how do you choose? Despite advertisers' claims and the huge discrepancy in the prices of shampoos, the basic job they all do is clean your hair. They accomplish this with a dilute mixture of detergent and water. Shampoos do vary, though—those for oily hair contain stronger detergents, those for dry or damaged hair use gentler ones.

Think about what your hair is like and what it needs before you buy a shampoo. Dandruff shampoos to relieve itchy or flaky scalps have been around for decades. There are also newer products that can add moisture or volume to dry or limp hair, protect the color of dyed hair, or gently clean hair that has already been processed with straighteners or permanents.

While shampooing strips away dirt, it can also rob your hair of too many natural oils, leaving it unmanageable and flyaway. Shampooing too often can also leave your hair dry and brittle. You may need to follow your shampoo with conditioner to replace some of the stripped-off oils and to detangle and moisturize your hair. Conditioners also coat and reinforce the hair shaft, enhancing its luster, the ability to reflect light.

Not all shampoos on the market are good for your hair. A good shampoo has a ph balance of 5-7. If you are uncertain about which shampoo or conditioner is right for your hair, consult a hairdresser.

For centuries, balsam products (which are fragrant oils) have been used in conditioners, but modern ingredients such as silicon work better. Silicon, for instance, deposits itself in thin layers on the hair shaft, softening and protecting it without weighing it down.

Don't use too much conditioner. For short hair use less than a tablespoon, and for long hair apply it only from your ears down. If convenience is important to you, you can buy products that combine shampoo and conditioner.

To keep your hair shiny and beautiful, you must also protect it from damaging external elements. These include the sun (UV rays can alter your hair's protein structures), wind, saltwater, chlorine, and extreme temperatures. Although sunscreens are appearing in more and more hair care products, to protect your hair from the sun and harsh weather, nothing beats a hat. After swimming in the sea or a chlorinated pool, rinse your hair well.

Proceed with caution before you subject you hair to harsh chemical processes such as using permanent waves, dyes, or straighteners. These products can be very damaging if they are handled incorrectly, and their overuse is a major mistake, says Philip Kingsley. If you are considering using these kinds of hair treatments, he suggests that you only use one process—the one that makes you look and feel best. Don't abuse your hair just to follow the newest fad.

If you decide to color your hair, you'll have lots of company. When Clairol first introduced "Instant Clairol Oil Shampoo Tint," a French product, to the United States in 1931, dyeing one's hair was a very risqué thing to do—thought of as most suited to actresses and women of ill repute. Clairol never even mentioned the word "dye" in their original advertisements. By the 1950s, though, attitudes about the practice relaxed, and large numbers of American women did begin to color their hair. Today, Clairol estimates that 48 percent of all American women do so.

Hair color products for use at home have become much easier in the past decade or so. Until about the 1980s, women had to slather their heads with smelly, tar-like goo, and they often wound up with hair that looked unnatural. Through continual improvements in the chemistry employed, today's fast-acting shampoos, gels, and creams feel and smell pleasant and produce more natural results than ever.

Today's dyes fall into four main categories, giving consumers a lot of choices:

- Temporary: Available since the 1930s, these colors, also called rinses, coat the cuticle without penetrating it. They wash out after one shampoo.

- Semipermanent: First introduced by Clairol in 1961, these dyes are usually applied like shampoo and coat the hair shaft with color. They may slightly penetrate it to deposit dye between the cuticle and cortex. They wash away after six to twelve shampoos, making them a good choice if you're not sure about the color you're choosing or just want to look different for a while.

- Tone-on-tone (or demipermanent): The newest category of hair colors, introduced by L'Oreal in 1993, these dyes penetrate the cuticle and cortex but do not alter the natural pigment. Instead they blend a complementary tone with the natural color to enhance and brighten it. Since they don't remove the hair's own color, new growth at the roots isn't so obvious. They wash out after about twenty-eight shampoos.

- Permanent: These hair color products, available since 1931, are a bigger commitment to a new look. They remove the natural pigment from your hair and replace it with dye. To do this, they open the scales of the cuticle like a venetian blind, which allows the new color to enter the hair shaft. A strong chemical called peroxide, found in most permanent dyes,

This little girl's hair has been tightly braided, and is probably much longer that it appears. Different cultures from around the world have produced many varied styles and fashions.

removes the hair's natural pigment from the cortex, the hair's outer layer. Then the artificial colors can be deposited on the cortex like paint on a blank wall. Inside the cortex, the dye molecule undergoes a chemical reaction that enlarges it, trapping the new color inside. Permanent dyes alter your hair color for good, but new hair that grows in exhibits your natural shade. Treatments must be repeated to tint the roots and to freshen the dye all along the shaft.

Giving yourself a "perm" (short for permanent), or having one done in a salon, is another route to a very different look. It is permanent because the only way to completely get rid of it is to grow it out. Perms work in two stages. First, you apply a waving solution to your hair to break down the chemical bonds that usually determine its straightness or waviness. With those bonds broken, your hair shafts swell. Step two uses a special chemical called a neutralizer and perm rods, which look like curlers, to rebuild the bonds, locking in new waves or curls.

When people with very curly hair choose to straighten it, the process is the same. After the initial solution is applied to break the hair's natural bonds, a neutralizer is applied to rebuild the bonds in a new way, in this case, straight.

Hair that has been treated by a perm or straightener retains its new shape permanently. If you want to keep the changed look, though, further treatments must be done to alter the new growth. If you use a perm or straightener, take great care to follow instructions on the package.

Shampooing and conditioning your hair well and protecting it from too many external assaults are the basic steps to maintain the beauty of the hair that's now on your head. To make sure the hair that is yet to emerge also looks its best too, you must eat wisely. Gaps in your nutrition—especially too few proteins and carbohydrates—can disrupt your hair's growth. For example, anorexics who starve themselves often have very thin hair. So strive for a balanced diet.

Caring for the hair on your head is one kind of beauty challenge. Getting rid of unwanted hair is another. Actually, although American women prize smooth underarms and silky legs, women in many other parts of the world don't. In fact, some Mediterranean cultures even consider a mustache on a woman sexy.

For unwanted hair on your legs and underarms, shaving is the simplest, fastest, and least costly answer. Straight-edged razors, long blades attached to handles like the ones barbers use, have been around for thousands of years. Safety razors, small, disposable blades shielded by plastic or metal holders, are a relatively recent invention.

The Gillette Company first started selling small razors with disposable blades in 1904 (back then twenty blades cost $1.00). Gillette also introduced the first razor especially for women in 1915. Their advertisements for a lady's razor never used the term "shaving." Back then, men shaved; women merely "smoothed." The disposable razors that are popular now first reached the market in 1975. Razors that use disposable blades are a better choice if you want to reduce pollution and waste.

When you shave your legs, don't begin the minute you

enter the bath or shower. If you wait a few minutes, the hair soaks up water, softening it and making it easier to remove.

Depilatories offer another option for hair removal. These products contain strong chemicals that weaken and dissolve hairs, which can then be washed away. They remove hair closer to the skin than razors do, so the results can be very smooth. But they can be expensive to use on large areas, and some people dislike the messiness and harsh smells involved.

Waxing removes hair by applying melted wax to the skin and letting it harden. Then, when the wax is quickly pulled off, hairs come out with it. Waxing can leave skin smooth for three to six weeks, but it can be painful, costly (especially if you have it done at a salon), and irritating. Also, since hair has to grow out again before the process can be repeated, you have to put up with a stubbly period between treatments.

Electrolysis was, until recently, the only permanent method for removing hair. It has been used mainly to eliminate hair from small areas like the upper lip or chin. A skilled practitioner uses a small needle-like probe that is connected to a machine that produces electric currents. The practitioner inserts the probe into individual hair follicles and briefly turns on the current. When the electricity runs through the needle into the hair, it kills it at the root. Many return visits to the practitioner's office may be required. Electrolysis can be both costly and uncomfortable.

Before undergoing electrolysis, be sure that you've found a highly skilled person. The best source of a referral is a dermatologist. An unskilled person can leave you with serious permanent scars.

In 1996, a new laser-based system for long-lasting hair removal made its debut. Thermo-Lase's Soft Light Hair-Removal System received FDA approval in 1995. How it works: First the area to be treated is waxed to remove hairs, leaving the follicles empty. Then a special black heat-conducting lotion is applied to the skin and penetrates the hair follicles. When a laser is shined on the area, the black lotion absorbs its energy, causing heat that damages those parts of the hair involved in growth. No damage results to other parts of the skin.

For most people, the laser treatments cause only a tingling or a sensation of warmth. Some others feel as though rubber bands are being snapped against their skin. The few side effects that seldom occur--slight redness, tightness, or the feeling of a mild sunburn--usually pass within a few hours.

Laser-based hair removal requires several treatments since it only destroys hairs that are growing, not those that are resting or dying. Since the laser scans whole areas of the body, it is much faster than electrolysis, which destroys hairs one by one. Since a medical practitioner must administer the procedure, the new treatment is quite expensive.

In 1992, the FDA also approved the first anesthetic (numbing) cream that can reduce the pain involved in waxing or electrolysis. It's called EMLA, for Eutectic Mixture of Local Anesthetic. Eutectic means that the mixture melts more easily than either of the two drugs in it would melt by itself. The two anesthetic drugs are lidocaine and prilocaine. A local anesthetic is one that works only within a defined area of the body, unlike a general anesthetic, which makes you unconscious so you won't feel pain. EMLA, which is available by pre-scription, needs to be applied to the area to be treated about an hour in advance.

Whether you want to make the hair framing your face a pleasure to feel and see, or you want to eliminate hair where you'd rather be smooth, you have more choices today than ever before. Understand your hair, and you'll choose well.

Carmen's hairdresser took the time to talk with Carmen and show her photos of many flattering styles she could wear that would emphasize the prettiness of her naturally thick dark curls. She told Carmen to use deep conditioners and gentle styling techniques to minimize the damage she had already done, and she cut Carmen's hair into an attrac-tive style to wear while her new hair grew in. Eighteen months after her disastrous run-in with the bleach and straightener, Carmen looked great . . . with a stylish head full of shiny, dark curls.　　　　　　　　　　◆

AFTERWORD

Keeping Beauty in Perspective

You have seen, by reading this book, that beauty has concerned people throughout history. One feature that distinguishes our age, though, is the great power that mass media have to influence our ideas about beauty and our feelings about ourselves.

It's vital to keep beauty in perspective. You can strive to look good and feel confident about yourself without making your appearance the focus of your life. Dr. Mary Pipher is a psychologist who has worked closely with adolescents for decades. The author of *Reviving Ophelia: Saving the Selves of Adolescent Girls*, she offers these suggestions:

1. Choose the media you consume with care. Avoid music,

magazines, or TV shows with the message that the only important thing about a girl or boy is his or her body.

2. Stop discussing your weight and looks with friends. Make a pact with your friends to drop those subjects for a month.

3. Never tease another kid about appearances.

4. Be careful who you befriend. If your current friends are obsessed with looks, seek others who you can respect more. Try to spend some time with people of different age groups too—they'll share different life perspectives that can be empowering.

5. Volunteer—helping others will let you feel good about your inner self. It's an eye-opener too—worrying about your thighs seems silly when you work with people who cannot walk.

6. Set your sights on goals you can control. You can't transform yourself into a model or the most popular person. But you can decide who you'll befriend and how you use your time. Develop your interests and talents—work toward important goals.   ◆

Glossary

aesthetic: pertaining to what is beautiful.

Automated Lamellar Keratoplasty (ALK): an operation used to correct both near- and farsightedness. In ALK, a thin layer of the cornea is removed, improving the eye's ability to focus light on the retina.

bone density: a measure of the solidity and strength of bones.

carotene: an orange or red substance that occurs in carrots and other vegetables.

cataracts: a cloudy area in the lens of the eye, which causes a gradual, painless loss of vision.

contraceptives: methods used to prevent pregnancy.

cortisone: a hormone made by the adrenal glands (which sit on the kidneys), or a man-made version of this hormone.

DNA: a complex protein found in cells; it controls cells and creatures made of cells in two ways. First, it passes on hereditary information from one generation of cells to the next. Second, it controls the cells' production of protein.

ethnicity: people grouped together according to common racial, national, tribal, religious, linguistic, or cultural origin or background.

gender: a person's sex.

hormone: a powerful substance produced within the body and then carried by blood to an organ it stimulates. Hormones may be made synthetically.

hyperopia: farsightedness, a visual disorder in which far objects are seen clearly and close objects appear blurry.

immune system: those bodily organs that work together to protect the body from disease-causing organisms and other foreign bodies.

infectious diseases: illnesses caused by the growth of disease-producing microorganisms in the body. Infectious diseases may be spread from one person to another by contact or close association.

intercourse: physical act of sexual union between a man and a woman.

keratin: a tough protein found in the skin's epidermis, in nails, hair, and tooth enamel.

keratinocytes: flat cells that comprise the top of the epidermis, named for the keratin they contain.

life expectancy: the number of years for which, according to statistical predictions, a person may expect to live.

melanin: the dark pigment that is found in skin, hair, and the iris of the eye.

melanoma: a cancerous tumor formed from a pigment-bearing cell in the skin (a melanocyte). The main cause of melanoma is excess exposure to the sun's UV rays.

myopia: nearsightedness, a visual disorder in which near objects are seen clearly and faraway objects appear blurry.

optic nerve: the bundle of fibers that carry visual information from the eye to the brain, where it is processed.

ozone layer: a region of the atmosphere with a high ozone content, about twenty-five miles above ground. It serves as an important filter to block some of the sun's harmful UV rays from reaching the earth.

puberty: the life stage at which a person becomes reproductively mature, capable of having offspring.

side effect: a secondary, and usually unwanted, effect of a drug that occurs along with its intended effect.

sunblocks: also called sunscreens, these products act to reduce the harmful effects of the sun's ultraviolet rays upon the skin.

radial keratotomy (RK): an operation used to correct moderate nearsightedness or astigmatism. In RK, spoke-shaped slits cut in the cornea improve its ability to focus light on the retina.

Activity Section

HOW FAST DO FINGERNAILS GROW?

Did you ever hear your friends complain about their fingernails? They grow too fast or too slow, break or chip easily, or only look good in the summer. Try a fingernail experiment to test different questions you may have about how fingernails grow. Brainstorm different hypotheses to test: Do fingernails grow faster if you have nail polish on them? Do younger children's nails grow faster than teenagers' nails? Do fingernails on different hands grow at different rates? Does eating a certain food affect fingernail growth? Make a prediction, and then begin!

When you have decided on the question you would like to test, you'll need these basic materials: a ruler with 1/16 or 1mm divisions, at least 5 sheets of graph paper, and other materials, such as nail polish, depending on your test.

Designate one piece of graph paper for each finger (i.e., index fingers for left and right hand can be graphed on the same paper). Measure the length of each fingernail and record it on the appropriate graph. Measure your nails every day at the same time for two weeks (or a designated number of days), and record results on your graph.

What were your results? Display your graphs and share them with your classmates. Explain why you think you ended up with certain results.

HOW WELL ARE YOU CARING FOR YOUR TEETH?

Do this simple test to see how well you're doing removing plaque with your toothbrush. You'll need a toothbrush and two disclosing tablets per person, plus a tube of toothpaste, a mirror, cups of water, and a sink. Brush your teeth like you would on a normal night. Chew the disclosing tablet and inspect. How well did you do? Brush again, especially around the spots you missed and do a second inspection. This experiment may surprise you, and could very well prevent your next filling!

Index